50 Samurai Sweet Tooth Recipes

By: Kelly Johnson

Table of Contents

- **Yokan** (Sweet Red Bean Jelly)
- **Mizu Yokan** (Soft, Water-Based Yokan)
- **Dorayaki** (Red Bean-Filled Pancakes)
- **Kuzumochi** (Arrowroot Jelly Mochi)
- **Warabi Mochi** (Bracken Starch Jelly with Kinako)
- **Dango** (Sweet Rice Dumplings on a Stick)
- **Hanami Dango** (Tri-Colored Flower Viewing Dango)
- **Mitarashi Dango** (Soy Glaze Rice Dumplings)
- **Anmitsu** (Sweet Red Bean and Jelly Dessert)
- **Oshiruko** (Sweet Red Bean Soup with Mochi)
- **Zenzai** (Thicker Red Bean Soup)
- **Taiyaki** (Fish-Shaped Pastry with Red Bean Filling)
- **Manju** (Steamed Sweet Bean-Filled Buns)
- **Kashiwa Mochi** (Oak-Wrapped Mochi with Sweet Filling)
- **Sakura Mochi** (Cherry Blossom-Flavored Mochi)
- **Botamochi** (Glutinous Rice Coated with Sweet Beans)
- **Ohagi** (Autumn Version of Botamochi)
- **Karukan** (Steamed Yam Cake)
- **Shiratama Zenzai** (Sweet Rice Flour Dumplings in Red Bean Soup)
- **Higashi** (Dry, Powdered Sugar Wagashi)
- **Rakugan** (Pressed Sugar and Rice Flour Sweets)
- **Monaka** (Crispy Wafers with Red Bean Filling)
- **Amanatto** (Candied Sweet Beans)
- **Hoshigaki** (Dried Persimmons)
- **Daifuku** (Soft Mochi with Sweet Bean Filling)
- **Ichigo Daifuku** (Mochi Filled with Red Bean and Strawberry)
- **Mizu Manju** (Translucent Jelly-Like Sweet with Red Bean)
- **Uiro** (Steamed Rice Flour Cake)
- **Joyo Manju** (Soft Yam-Based Sweet Bun)
- **Kintsuba** (Red Bean Paste Covered in a Light Batter)
- **Yatsuhashi** (Cinnamon-Flavored Rice Crackers)
- **Fukashi** (Steamed Sweet Bread)
- **Tsubuan Mochi** (Mochi with Chunky Sweet Bean Paste)
- **Imo Yokan** (Sweet Potato Jelly)
- **Kaki Yokan** (Persimmon-Flavored Sweet Jelly)

- **Miso Manju** (Sweet Bun with Miso-Flavored Filling)
- **Inaka Manju** (Rustic Steamed Bun with Sweet Bean Paste)
- **Kuzuyu** (Hot Kudzu Starch Sweet Drink)
- **Tsukigesho** (Moon-Themed Sweet Cake)
- **Kiku no Kanten** (Chrysanthemum-Shaped Agar Jelly)
- **Kuro Ame** (Traditional Black Sugar Candy)
- **Fuku Manju** (Lucky Fortune Sweet Buns)
- **Goma Dango** (Sesame-Covered Sweet Rice Dumplings)
- **Kinako Mochi** (Toasted Soybean Flour-Dusted Mochi)
- **Kusa Mochi** (Mugwort-Flavored Mochi)
- **Hakka Ame** (Peppermint Hard Candy)
- **Yokan Maki** (Rolled Sweet Bean Jelly)
- **Nerikiri** (Handcrafted Artistic Wagashi)
- **Shogoin Yatsuhashi** (Soft Cinnamon Rice Cake)
- **Umeboshi Kanroni** (Sweet Pickled Plums in Syrup)

Yokan (Sweet Red Bean Jelly)

Ingredients

- 1 cup red bean paste (anko)
- 1 1/2 cups water
- 2 tsp agar-agar powder
- 1/4 cup sugar

Instructions

1. Dissolve agar-agar in water and bring to a boil.
2. Add sugar and red bean paste, stirring until smooth.
3. Pour into a mold and let set in the fridge.
4. Slice and serve.

Mizu Yokan (Soft, Water-Based Yokan)

Ingredients

- 1 cup red bean paste (anko)
- 2 cups water
- 1 1/2 tsp agar-agar powder
- 1/4 cup sugar

Instructions

1. Dissolve agar-agar in water and bring to a boil.
2. Add sugar and red bean paste, stirring until fully dissolved.
3. Pour into a mold and let cool before refrigerating.
4. Slice and serve chilled.

Dorayaki (Red Bean-Filled Pancakes)

Ingredients

- 1 cup all-purpose flour
- 1/2 cup sugar
- 1/2 tsp baking powder
- 2 eggs
- 1/2 cup water
- 1/2 cup sweet red bean paste (anko)

Instructions

1. Mix flour, sugar, baking powder, eggs, and water into a batter.
2. Cook small pancakes on a non-stick pan until golden.
3. Spread red bean paste between two pancakes and serve.

Kuzumochi (Arrowroot Jelly Mochi)

Ingredients

- 1/2 cup kuzu starch
- 2 cups water
- 1/4 cup sugar
- Kinako (roasted soybean flour), for dusting

Instructions

1. Mix kuzu starch, water, and sugar in a saucepan over low heat.
2. Stir until it thickens and turns translucent.
3. Pour into a mold and let cool.
4. Slice and dust with kinako before serving.

Warabi Mochi (Bracken Starch Jelly with Kinako)

Ingredients

- 1/2 cup warabi starch
- 2 cups water
- 1/4 cup sugar
- Kinako (roasted soybean flour), for dusting

Instructions

1. Mix warabi starch, water, and sugar in a saucepan.
2. Heat and stir until it thickens and turns translucent.
3. Pour into a mold and let cool.
4. Cut into bite-sized pieces and coat with kinako.

Dango (Sweet Rice Dumplings on a Stick)

Ingredients

- 1 cup mochiko (sweet rice flour)
- 1/2 cup warm water
- 1 tbsp sugar

Instructions

1. Mix mochiko, water, and sugar into a smooth dough.
2. Roll into small balls and boil until they float.
3. Skewer onto sticks and serve.

Hanami Dango (Tri-Colored Flower Viewing Dango)

Ingredients

- 1 cup mochiko (sweet rice flour)
- 1/2 cup warm water
- 1 tbsp sugar
- Food coloring (pink and green)

Instructions

1. Mix mochiko, water, and sugar into a smooth dough.
2. Divide into three portions, coloring one pink and one green.
3. Roll into small balls and boil until they float.
4. Skewer in alternating colors and serve.

Mitarashi Dango (Soy Glaze Rice Dumplings)

Ingredients

- 1 cup mochiko (sweet rice flour)
- 1/2 cup warm water
- 1 tbsp sugar
- 2 tbsp soy sauce
- 1 tbsp sugar
- 1/2 tbsp mirin

Instructions

1. Mix mochiko, water, and sugar into a smooth dough.
2. Roll into small balls and boil until they float.
3. Skewer onto sticks.
4. Simmer soy sauce, sugar, and mirin to make a glaze.
5. Brush glaze over dango before serving.

Anmitsu (Sweet Red Bean and Jelly Dessert)

Ingredients

- 1/2 cup kanten (agar jelly), cubed
- 1/4 cup sweet red beans (anko)
- 1/2 cup fresh fruit (strawberries, mandarin oranges)
- 1 tbsp kuromitsu (brown sugar syrup)

Instructions

1. Arrange kanten, red beans, and fruit in a bowl.
2. Drizzle with kuromitsu before serving.

Oshiruko (Sweet Red Bean Soup with Mochi)

Ingredients

- 1 cup sweet red bean paste (anko)
- 2 cups water
- 2 mochi pieces

Instructions

1. Heat red bean paste with water, stirring until smooth.
2. Grill mochi until slightly crispy.
3. Serve warm with mochi.

Zenzai (Thicker Red Bean Soup)

Ingredients

- 1 cup sweet red bean paste (anko)
- 2 cups water
- 2 mochi pieces

Instructions

1. Heat red bean paste with water, stirring until thickened.
2. Grill mochi until slightly crispy.
3. Serve warm with mochi pieces in the soup.

Taiyaki (Fish-Shaped Pastry with Red Bean Filling)

Ingredients

- 1 cup all-purpose flour
- 1/2 tsp baking powder
- 1 tbsp sugar
- 3/4 cup water
- 1/2 cup sweet red bean paste (anko)

Instructions

1. Mix flour, baking powder, sugar, and water into a smooth batter.
2. Heat a taiyaki mold and pour in batter, then add red bean paste.
3. Cover with more batter and cook until golden brown on both sides.

Manju (Steamed Sweet Bean-Filled Buns)

Ingredients

- 1 cup all-purpose flour
- 1/2 tsp baking powder
- 1/4 cup sugar
- 1/4 cup water
- 1/2 cup sweet red bean paste (anko)

Instructions

1. Mix flour, baking powder, sugar, and water into a smooth dough.
2. Divide and flatten dough into small circles.
3. Place red bean paste in the center and seal.
4. Steam for 10 minutes until fluffy.

Kashiwa Mochi (Oak-Wrapped Mochi with Sweet Filling)

Ingredients

- 1 cup mochiko (sweet rice flour)
- 1/2 cup water
- 1/2 cup sweet red bean paste (anko)
- 4 kashiwa (oak) leaves (for wrapping)

Instructions

1. Mix mochiko and water into a smooth dough.
2. Steam until sticky, then knead until smooth.
3. Divide dough and wrap around red bean paste.
4. Wrap each mochi with an oak leaf and serve.

Sakura Mochi (Cherry Blossom-Flavored Mochi)

Ingredients

- 1 cup mochiko (sweet rice flour)
- 1/2 cup water
- 1 tbsp sugar
- 1/2 cup sweet red bean paste (anko)
- 4 pickled sakura leaves (for wrapping)

Instructions

1. Mix mochiko, sugar, and water into a smooth batter.
2. Cook small pancakes on a non-stick pan.
3. Wrap red bean paste in pancakes and fold over.
4. Wrap each piece with a sakura leaf.

Botamochi (Glutinous Rice Coated with Sweet Beans)

Ingredients

- 1 cup glutinous rice
- 1 1/2 cups water
- 1/2 cup sweet red bean paste (anko)

Instructions

1. Cook glutinous rice with water until soft.
2. Mash lightly while keeping some texture.
3. Shape into small balls and coat with red bean paste.

Ohagi (Autumn Version of Botamochi)

Ingredients

- 1 cup glutinous rice
- 1 1/2 cups water
- 1/2 cup sweet red bean paste (anko)

Instructions

1. Cook glutinous rice with water until soft.
2. Mash lightly while keeping some texture.
3. Shape into small balls and coat with red bean paste.

Karukan (Steamed Yam Cake)

Ingredients

- 1/2 cup grated Japanese yam (nagaimo)
- 1 cup rice flour
- 1/2 cup sugar
- 1/2 cup water

Instructions

1. Mix grated yam, rice flour, sugar, and water into a batter.
2. Pour into a mold and steam for 15 minutes until firm.

Shiratama Zenzai (Sweet Rice Flour Dumplings in Red Bean Soup)

Ingredients

- 1 cup sweet red bean paste (anko)
- 2 cups water
- 1/2 cup shiratama flour (glutinous rice flour)
- 1/4 cup water (for dumplings)

Instructions

1. Mix shiratama flour and water into a smooth dough.
2. Roll into small balls and boil until they float.
3. Heat red bean paste with water to make a soup.
4. Serve dumplings in the soup.

Higashi (Dry, Powdered Sugar Wagashi)

Ingredients

- 1/2 cup glutinous rice flour
- 1/2 cup powdered sugar
- 1 tbsp water

Instructions

1. Mix rice flour and powdered sugar, then add water.
2. Press mixture into small molds and let dry completely before serving.

Rakugan (Pressed Sugar and Rice Flour Sweets)

Ingredients

- 1/2 cup glutinous rice flour
- 1/2 cup powdered sugar
- 1 tbsp water

Instructions

1. Mix rice flour and powdered sugar, then add water.
2. Press mixture into small molds.
3. Let dry completely before serving.

Monaka (Crispy Wafers with Red Bean Filling)

Ingredients

- 6 monaka wafers (store-bought or homemade)
- 1/2 cup sweet red bean paste (anko)

Instructions

1. Spread red bean paste inside one monaka wafer.
2. Press another wafer on top to form a sandwich.
3. Serve immediately to keep wafers crispy.

Amanatto (Candied Sweet Beans)

Ingredients

- 1 cup azuki beans
- 1/2 cup sugar
- 1/2 cup water

Instructions

1. Soak azuki beans overnight, then boil until soft.
2. Simmer in sugar syrup for 30 minutes.
3. Drain and let dry before serving.

Hoshigaki (Dried Persimmons)

Ingredients

- 4 ripe persimmons

Instructions

1. Peel persimmons and hang them in a dry, sunny place for 4–6 weeks.
2. Massage gently every few days to help sugars develop.
3. Serve once they are dried and slightly white from natural sugars.

Daifuku (Soft Mochi with Sweet Bean Filling)

Ingredients

- 1 cup mochiko (sweet rice flour)
- 1/2 cup water
- 1/4 cup sugar
- 1/2 cup sweet red bean paste (anko)
- Cornstarch (for dusting)

Instructions

1. Mix mochiko, sugar, and water into a smooth batter.
2. Steam until sticky, then knead until smooth.
3. Dust hands with cornstarch and wrap mochi around red bean paste.

Ichigo Daifuku (Mochi Filled with Red Bean and Strawberry)

Ingredients

- 1 cup mochiko (sweet rice flour)
- 1/2 cup water
- 1/4 cup sugar
- 1/2 cup sweet red bean paste (anko)
- 4 strawberries
- Cornstarch (for dusting)

Instructions

1. Mix mochiko, sugar, and water into a smooth batter.
2. Steam until sticky, then knead until smooth.
3. Flatten mochi, place red bean paste and a strawberry inside, and seal.

Mizu Manju (Translucent Jelly-Like Sweet with Red Bean)

Ingredients

- 1/2 cup kuzu starch
- 2 cups water
- 1/4 cup sugar
- 1/2 cup sweet red bean paste (anko)

Instructions

1. Mix kuzu starch, water, and sugar in a saucepan.
2. Heat and stir until it thickens and turns translucent.
3. Pour half into molds, add red bean paste, then top with more mixture.
4. Chill until set before serving.

Uiro (Steamed Rice Flour Cake)

Ingredients

- 1 cup rice flour
- 1/2 cup sugar
- 1 cup water

Instructions

1. Mix rice flour, sugar, and water into a smooth batter.
2. Pour into a mold and steam for 30 minutes.
3. Cool, slice, and serve.

Joyo Manju (Soft Yam-Based Sweet Bun)

Ingredients

- 1/2 cup grated yam (nagaimo)
- 1 cup rice flour
- 1/4 cup sugar
- 1/2 cup sweet red bean paste (anko)

Instructions

1. Mix grated yam, rice flour, and sugar into a dough.
2. Divide dough into small circles and wrap around red bean paste.
3. Steam for 15 minutes and serve warm.

Kintsuba (Red Bean Paste Covered in a Light Batter)

Ingredients

- 1 cup sweet red bean paste (anko)
- 1/2 cup all-purpose flour
- 1/2 cup water
- 1 tbsp sugar

Instructions

1. Shape red bean paste into squares and chill until firm.
2. Mix flour, water, and sugar into a smooth batter.
3. Coat the red bean squares lightly with batter.
4. Pan-fry each side until golden brown.

Yatsuhashi (Cinnamon-Flavored Rice Crackers)

Ingredients

- 1/2 cup rice flour
- 1/4 cup sugar
- 1/2 tsp cinnamon
- 1/4 cup water

Instructions

1. Mix rice flour, sugar, cinnamon, and water into a dough.
2. Roll thinly and cut into rectangles.
3. Bake at 350°F (175°C) for 10–12 minutes until crisp.

Fukashi (Steamed Sweet Bread)

Ingredients

- 1 cup all-purpose flour
- 1/2 cup sugar
- 1 tsp baking powder
- 1/2 cup water

Instructions

1. Mix flour, sugar, baking powder, and water into a batter.
2. Pour into a mold and steam for 20 minutes.
3. Let cool before slicing.

Tsubuan Mochi (Mochi with Chunky Sweet Bean Paste)

Ingredients

- 1 cup mochiko (sweet rice flour)
- 1/2 cup water
- 1/4 cup sugar
- 1/2 cup chunky red bean paste (tsubuan)
- Cornstarch (for dusting)

Instructions

1. Mix mochiko, sugar, and water into a smooth batter.
2. Steam until sticky, then knead until smooth.
3. Shape into small balls and coat with chunky red bean paste.

Imo Yokan (Sweet Potato Jelly)

Ingredients

- 1 cup sweet potato, steamed and mashed
- 1/2 cup water
- 2 tsp agar-agar powder
- 1/4 cup sugar

Instructions

1. Dissolve agar-agar in water and bring to a boil.
2. Add sugar and mashed sweet potato, mixing until smooth.
3. Pour into a mold and chill until set.

Kaki Yokan (Persimmon-Flavored Sweet Jelly)

Ingredients

- 1 cup persimmon puree
- 1/2 cup water
- 2 tsp agar-agar powder
- 1/4 cup sugar

Instructions

1. Dissolve agar-agar in water and bring to a boil.
2. Add sugar and persimmon puree, stirring until smooth.
3. Pour into a mold and chill until set.

Miso Manju (Sweet Bun with Miso-Flavored Filling)

Ingredients

- 1 cup all-purpose flour
- 1/2 tsp baking powder
- 1/4 cup sugar
- 1/2 cup water
- 1/4 cup sweet miso paste

Instructions

1. Mix flour, baking powder, sugar, and water into a smooth dough.
2. Divide and flatten dough into small circles.
3. Place sweet miso paste in the center and seal.
4. Steam for 15 minutes.

Inaka Manju (Rustic Steamed Bun with Sweet Bean Paste)

Ingredients

- 1 cup all-purpose flour
- 1/2 tsp baking powder
- 1/4 cup sugar
- 1/2 cup water
- 1/2 cup sweet red bean paste (anko)

Instructions

1. Mix flour, baking powder, sugar, and water into a smooth dough.
2. Divide and flatten dough into small circles.
3. Place red bean paste in the center and seal.
4. Steam for 15 minutes.

Kuzuyu (Hot Kudzu Starch Sweet Drink)

Ingredients

- 1 tbsp kudzu starch
- 1 cup water
- 1 tbsp sugar

Instructions

1. Mix kudzu starch with water in a saucepan.
2. Heat and stir continuously until thickened.
3. Serve warm.

Tsukigesho (Moon-Themed Sweet Cake)

Ingredients

- 1 cup all-purpose flour
- 1/2 cup sugar
- 1/2 tsp baking powder
- 1/2 cup white bean paste (shiroan)
- 1/2 cup water

Instructions

1. Mix flour, sugar, baking powder, and water into a smooth batter.
2. Form white bean paste into small balls.
3. Wrap batter around each ball and shape into a moon-like disc.
4. Bake at 350°F (175°C) for 10–12 minutes until lightly golden.

Kiku no Kanten (Chrysanthemum-Shaped Agar Jelly)

Ingredients

- 2 cups water
- 2 tsp agar-agar powder
- 1/4 cup sugar
- 1/4 tsp food coloring (yellow or pink)

Instructions

1. Dissolve agar-agar in water and bring to a boil.
2. Stir in sugar and food coloring, then pour into a chrysanthemum-shaped mold.
3. Let cool and set before serving.

Kuro Ame (Traditional Black Sugar Candy)

Ingredients

- 1 cup Okinawan black sugar
- 1/4 cup water
- 1/2 tsp soy sauce (optional)

Instructions

1. Heat black sugar and water in a saucepan over medium heat.
2. Stir continuously until thick and glossy.
3. Pour into molds and let cool until hardened.

Fuku Manju (Lucky Fortune Sweet Buns)

Ingredients

- 1 cup all-purpose flour
- 1/2 tsp baking powder
- 1/4 cup sugar
- 1/2 cup water
- 1/2 cup sweet red bean paste (anko)

Instructions

1. Mix flour, baking powder, sugar, and water into a smooth dough.
2. Divide and flatten dough into small circles.
3. Place red bean paste in the center and seal.
4. Steam for 15 minutes.

Goma Dango (Sesame-Covered Sweet Rice Dumplings)

Ingredients

- 1 cup mochiko (sweet rice flour)
- 1/2 cup water
- 1/4 cup sugar
- 1/2 cup black and white sesame seeds, mixed
- Oil for frying

Instructions

1. Mix mochiko, sugar, and water into a smooth dough.
2. Roll into small balls and coat with sesame seeds.
3. Deep-fry until golden brown.

Kinako Mochi (Toasted Soybean Flour-Dusted Mochi)

Ingredients

- 2 pieces mochi
- 1/4 cup kinako (roasted soybean flour)
- 1 tbsp sugar

Instructions

1. Toast mochi until slightly crispy.
2. Mix kinako and sugar, then coat mochi before serving.

Kusa Mochi (Mugwort-Flavored Mochi)

Ingredients

- 1 cup mochiko (sweet rice flour)
- 1/2 cup water
- 1/4 cup sugar
- 2 tbsp dried mugwort (yomogi), rehydrated and finely chopped
- 1/2 cup sweet red bean paste (anko) (optional)
- Cornstarch (for dusting)

Instructions

1. Mix mochiko, sugar, water, and mugwort into a smooth dough.
2. Steam until the mixture becomes sticky, then knead until smooth.
3. Shape into small balls or wrap around red bean paste.
4. Dust with cornstarch before serving.

Hakka Ame (Peppermint Hard Candy)

Ingredients

- 1 cup sugar
- 1/4 cup water
- 1/2 tsp peppermint extract

Instructions

1. Heat sugar and water in a saucepan over medium heat until it reaches 300°F (150°C).
2. Remove from heat and stir in peppermint extract.
3. Pour into molds and let cool until hardened.

Yokan Maki (Rolled Sweet Bean Jelly)

Ingredients

- 1 cup sweet red bean paste (anko)
- 1 1/2 cups water
- 2 tsp agar-agar powder
- 1/4 cup sugar
- 2 sheets nori (optional for rolling)

Instructions

1. Dissolve agar-agar in water and bring to a boil.
2. Stir in sugar and red bean paste, mixing until smooth.
3. Pour onto a flat tray and let cool slightly.
4. Roll into a log and slice before serving.

Nerikiri (Handcrafted Artistic Wagashi)

Ingredients

- 1 cup white bean paste (shiroan)
- 1/2 cup glutinous rice flour
- 1/4 cup sugar
- Food coloring (optional for designs)

Instructions

1. Mix white bean paste, rice flour, and sugar into a dough.
2. Knead until smooth and divide into portions.
3. Add food coloring and shape into flowers, leaves, or other intricate designs.
4. Serve as a delicate wagashi with tea.

Shogoin Yatsuhashi (Soft Cinnamon Rice Cake)

Ingredients

- 1/2 cup rice flour
- 1/4 cup sugar
- 1/2 cup water
- 1/2 tsp cinnamon
- 1/4 cup sweet red bean paste (anko)

Instructions

1. Mix rice flour, sugar, water, and cinnamon into a batter.
2. Steam until soft, then roll out into thin sheets.
3. Cut into squares and fold around red bean paste.

Umeboshi Kanroni (Sweet Pickled Plums in Syrup)

Ingredients

- 6 umeboshi (pickled plums)
- 1/2 cup sugar
- 1/2 cup water
- 1 tbsp mirin

Instructions

1. Simmer sugar, water, and mirin until slightly thickened.
2. Add umeboshi and simmer for 5 minutes.
3. Let cool before serving as a sweet and tangy treat.

www.ingramcontent.com/pod-product-compliance
Lightning Source LLC
LaVergne TN
LVHW081502060526
838201LV00056BA/2892